I0456471

FORAGED

# FORAGED

### POEMS OF
### HEALING + SPIRIT

RACHEL SIERRA

for the wanderer
who has found
their own path

foraged

i
have been
wearing
green

all of my
life

tell me,
how
do i
find
myself ?

camouflage

foraged

no matter
how i contort
myself

i can't seem
to thrive
here

foraged




like a
phantom limb
i ache
for a
place
i've not yet
found

foraged


i am a collage
of stories
people
cultures
before me

i am a lucky one

for my parents
and theirs
and theirs
and theirs

survived to pass
their lives
into my living body

never have i felt
the odds so small
for my existence

the branch of
the family tree
i embody

feels so wandering
so thin
so fortunate


delicate odds

foraged

loneliness

for a while,
now

foraged

the question isn't
where do i belong

but
to whom
do i belong

and who
belongs
to me?

foraged

i
am a
cultural
e q u a t i o n

$.25 + .25 + .25 + .25 \neq 1$

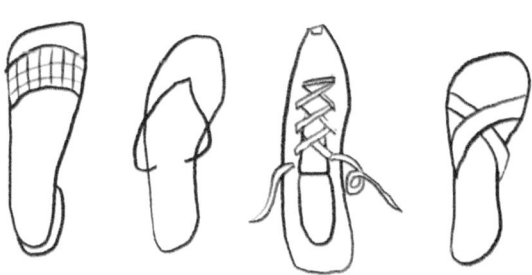

foraged

what is a home?

and

how many items
must be inside?

and

how many hours
must i spend within?

and

how many plants
must i collect?

and

how long
does it take
to grow roots?

a formula of belonging

foraged

the dusty
smell
of homecoming

reminds me

there will
always
be time

to rearrange
your interior
into a
more inhabitable
space

foraged

i am
back again
though
i am uncertain
to be here

the sun is testing
my limit
my boiling point

the house is sterile
rentable
but devoid of
my particular
disorder

but when i walked
the path by the sea

i felt the
heartbeat
of the waves
pounding the rocks

the sweet acidity of
rotting fruit

my muted footsteps
on the fallen
sea grape leaves

"i have missed you,"
said the land.
"your particular disorder."

foraged

having always
lived near
the ocean

there is something
about

homeostasis
in movement

that will
always
feel like
home

foraged

a fragment
cannot be
remade
into a whole

but i
have made
a mosaic
from the
pieces

foraged

my  belonging
will always
be an
art

foraged

i have been
an immigrant
everywhere
i have ever
lived

foraged

but what
do you call
a white immigrant

foraged

(expats do not exist)

foraged




sometimes i feel
so aware

that i am not
from here

so what right
do i have
to exist here

to take up
space
here

foraged

can you
tell me

(geographically)

where
i can
be
myself?

foraged

but if i
always
adapt

to every
environment

could someone
kindly
tell me

who
i
am?

a cultural chameleon

foraged

always feeling
i must
contort myself

into a million shapes
but my
natural one

that i am
disappointing
because i don't
have the same

experience
views
opinions

foraged


and yet
the land
remembers me

takes me in
as the orphan
that i am

and when my
hands are filled
with earth

how can i not
feel that

anything

planted in soil
can sprout
roots

foraged

no wonder
i am most at ease

outside

out there where
there is abundance

away from
people
noise
expectation

where all the
creatures
in their
natural habitats
thrive

and in so many words,
so do i

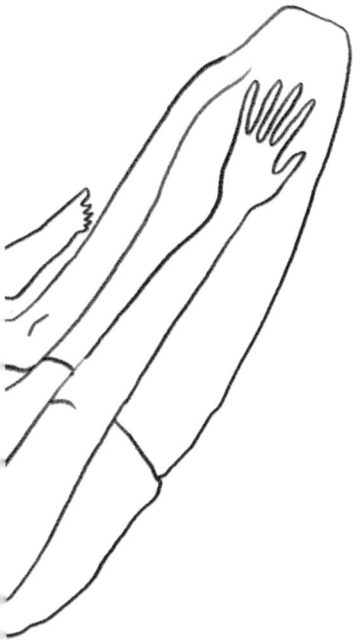

foraged

i have been
meditating
everyday

and it feels like

an opening
a heaviness
a smoothing

a hand pressed
against my
heart

pressure

foraged

i am walking
towards
my shadow

in hopes
of change

maybe
like clay
we both
can soften

be shaped
into something

curvier
smoother
more luscious

something to
hold
this expansion
this balm
this becoming

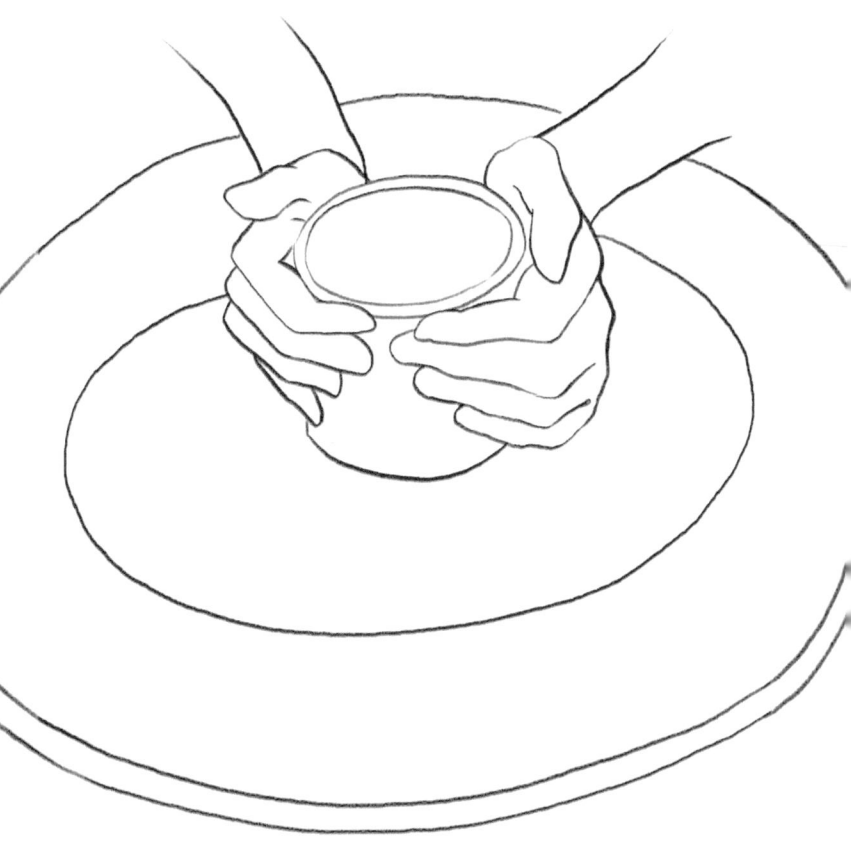

honey

don't ever
be ashamed
of your healing

not everything
happens quickly

but gently

you weren't ready
before

because your
time
is now

foraged

i need
living things
around me

as a
reminder
that
i, too
can thrive

foraged

my whole
life
has been
leading me
here

foraged

my entire
life's work

might be
just this:

to heal
myself
relentlessly

a full life

foraged

knowing that
my experience
would bring them
pain

knowing that
not being myself
brings me
pain

dilemma

foraged

my loyalty
is
killing
me

foraged

i am

_____

even if
people
don't believe me

i don't need to perform for love

foraged

when
they don't
see me

(i can see myself)

foraged

to only feel
loved
once i
see how
horrible
i am

repentance

foraged

i was
never
taught to
love
myself

how
do i
begin?

foraged

i am
becoming
everything
i ever
needed

foraged

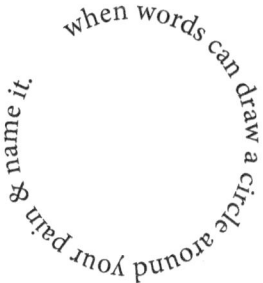

when words can draw a circle around your pain & name it.

foraged

contained

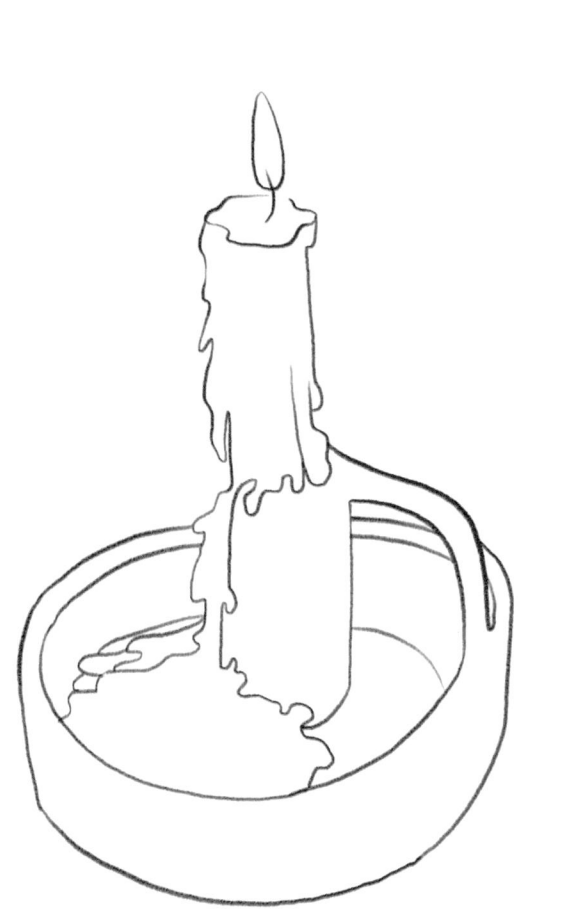

foraged

to my younger self:

you did what
you needed
to be loved

how could i
ever
hold that
against
you

the best you knew how

to be who
they want
would require
you to be
who you
are not


but to
want them
to change
would require
them to be
who they
are not


accept

foraged

how could
i tell you

self judgment
feels so
familiar
hard + safe

a place i can
return to

self forgiveness
feels so
foreign
soft + unstable

and it frightens me

foraged

as if
you could
spoil

anyone

with
too much
love

foraged

i
am
the
richest
person
i
know

mother
father
school
food
bed
house
car
electricity
water
safety

third world

foraged


i
am
the
poorest
person
i
know


hand me downs
thrift stores
coupons
guest rooms
bargain hunting
discount rack
donations
student loans
roommates
double shifts


first world

foraged

it's hard
to ask
for anything

when i am
surrounded
by
ravishing
poverty

thou shalt not want

foraged

i
do
not
want
to
want
anything

minimally human

it is hard
to be
a hero
and
a parent

so often
rescuing
and
saving
and fulfilling
your
destiny

not the
stay at home
type

and i would
never
ask you
to be


(but sometimes i still miss you)

foraged

two parents
without
great parents

came to parent
children
who had no
parents

but
(sometimes)
did not
parent
their own

a parentdox

foraged

rescuing
is your
love language

i used to
wish
i had a crisis

so you would
spend time
with me

~~but this is not~~ quality time

foraged

they needed
you
louder
than i
could ever
ask

volume

foraged

your
optimism
scared me

my anxiety
kept me
safe

foraged

please please

release
your grip
holding me
in the past

i cannot be
in two places
at once

i cannot be
who i once was

and

who i am now

without being
torn in half

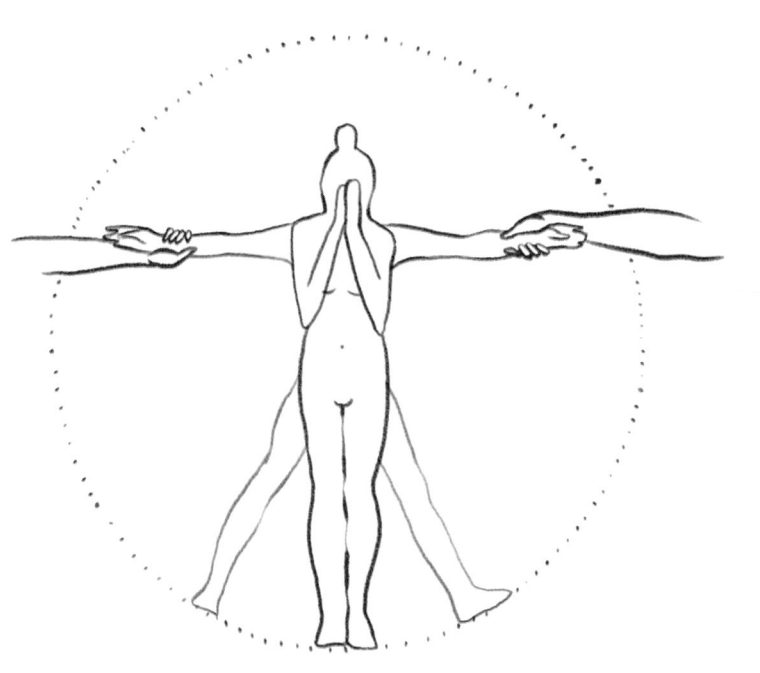

foraged




expansion

is

natural

is

right

foraged

but
if i didn't
get what i
needed


does that
make me
greedy


want

foraged

i won't
put myself
in a position
to be labeled

in other words:

unreasonable
illogical
feral

we speak
different
languages

and even if
you won't
understand it

doesn't mean
mine
is inferior

emotional

foraged

i don't want
to be nice

i want to
simply
be honest

foraged

i feel so

_____

when i rest

all my life
salvation
was found

in how much
i strove

when is it enough?

foraged

the scales
have been
tilted

and i
thought
it was
on me

to pull back
the tide
with the
gravity
that i am

but i
am not
the moon

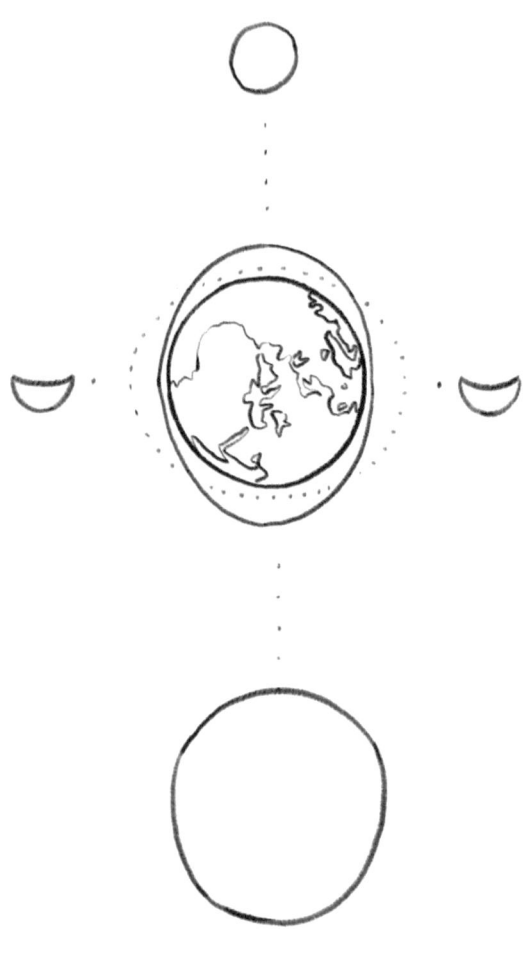

a tidal attraction

just because
you are not
interested

doesn't mean
i'm not
interesting

i'm f%@#ing fascinating

foraged

to jump off of a ship
that is on fire

to abandon
an ideal
that was scathing
to my soul

did not occur to me,

but
somewhere within
was a
self preservation
instinct

most would agree:
save yourself

yet sometimes,
less and less,
i still feel
an antiquated
almost romantic
idea

that i should have
gone down
with the
ship

survivors guilt / toxic christianity

foraged

evolving
does not
betray
anyone

but staying
small
betrays
yourself

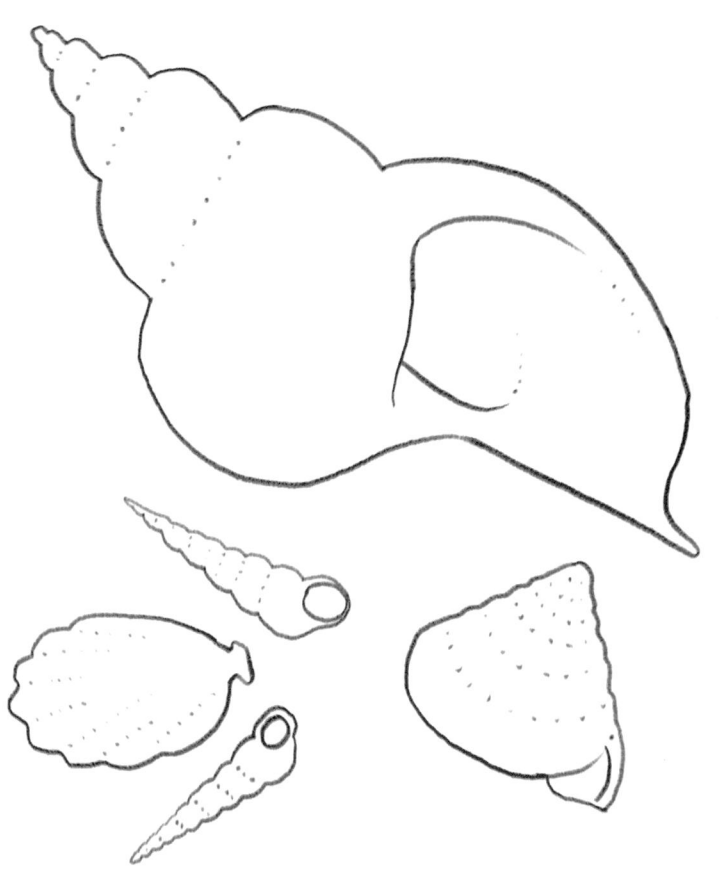

foraged

when you
were loyal
to something

all of your life

but it
did not
want
you

foraged

i carried
a spirituality
that was
never meant
to include
me

used

foraged

to be
taught
to not
trust
yourself

is
to be
taught

to not
be
whole

unforgivable

foraged

powerful men
have corporations

influential men
have platforms

principled men
have  churches


but a
strong woman
has no place
to rest her
head


a call to the wild

foraged

you are the
salt of the earth

but if you
lose your
taste

you are no longer
good for anything
except to be
thrown out

a salty woman

foraged

(do not)
let your light
shine
before men

so that they
(will not)
see your good works
(and feel inadequate)

on how to attract a husband

foraged

i wonder
how different
the story
would be

if the
victim
wrote
the narrative

maybe the
greatest
act of faith
would have been
to say
"no"

a problematic daddy

foraged

atonement violence

(is still violence)

choose the path of peace
choose the path of peace
choose the path of peace
choose the path of peace
choose the path of peace

foraged

mine
wasn't the
story
they wanted

it started
good
and ended
poorly

inconvenient
no redemption
no glory

so i went
elsewhere
and fashioned
a new home

i like it.

the end

foraged




but i still
don't know
how to reconcile

my religious heritage

with it's
colonialism
white saviorism
racism
sexism

foraged

by existing here
i feel
complicit

because
i have
benefited
from this

the problem is too big
the pieces too many
and i am so tired
from trying to salvage it

my entire lifetime
would not be long enough

and even if it was
it would make no difference

within this system
i am just one more woman
without a voice

foraged

and i'm
still not
interested

in normalizing
emotional
manipulation

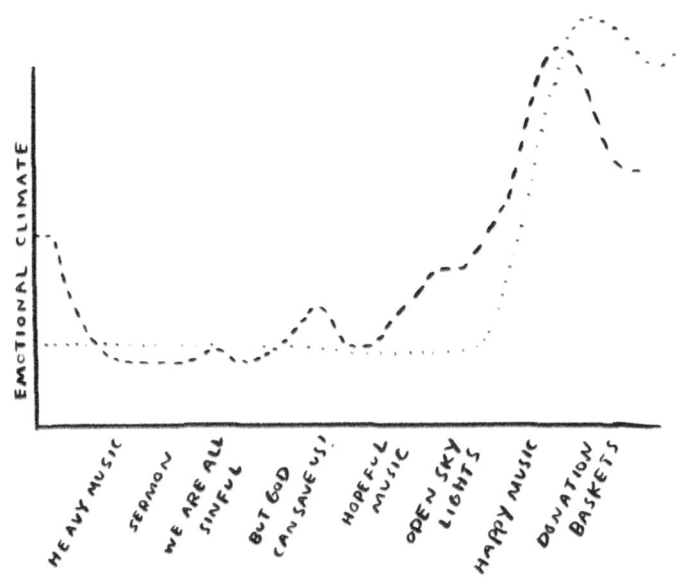

EMOTIONAL CLIMATE

HEAVY MUSIC
SERMON
WE ARE ALL SINFUL
BUT GOD CAN SAVE US!
HOPEFUL MUSIC
OPEN SKY LIGHTS
HAPPY MUSIC
DONATION BASKETS

--- = MECHANICS OF A SUNDAY

···· = FINANCES OF A SUNDAY

foraged


all the while
we were
in that
bleak little room

with it's sterile light
and brittle
plastic chairs

just out the window
the jungle pressed in

lush thick
nourishing
and alive

beckoning me
into that
overgrown abundance

so i crawled
out of church
by the back window

and out
into the dark
and fragrant night


exodus

foraged

i inherited
a tidy
spirituality:

crisp
sharp
two-toned

i was cut
by the edges

and
it could not
heal
what it  harmed

foraged




i foraged
my own
spirituality:

earth
and moss

flowers
and stones

rain
and light

a balm,
a river of delight

foraged




sometimes
i miss
feeling a
part of
something

foraged

but then
i remember:

i am a part
of this entire
cosmic
family

foraged

i have
only ever been
an
evangelist
of
beauty

foraged

when it rains
i feel
many
things

foraged


may my
tears
fall

medicinally

and when
i wake

i will
be
renewed




baptism

my spirituality is for me
my spirituality is for me
my spirituality is for me
my spirituality is for me

foraged

it is how
i love
this life
relentlessly

foraged

i give
myself
permission

foraged

today i behold
the abundance
that surrounds me

foraged

i have
mended
the leaks
to find
a river
a force
flowing
through me

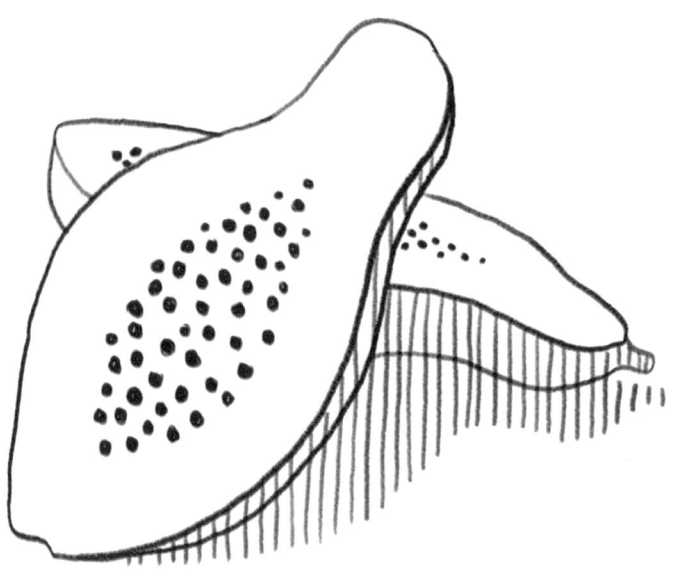

foraged

i am
urgently
grateful

(making up for lost time)

foraged

blessings

foraged

i am
healing
myself
for everyone
who could not
before
me

foraged

your pain
spilled over
to me

maybe
my healing
can
overflow
back to you

all of those
closed doors

- do not cry-

they were not
yours

your path
is deeper
still

descend
deeper
within

you will
find
your
way

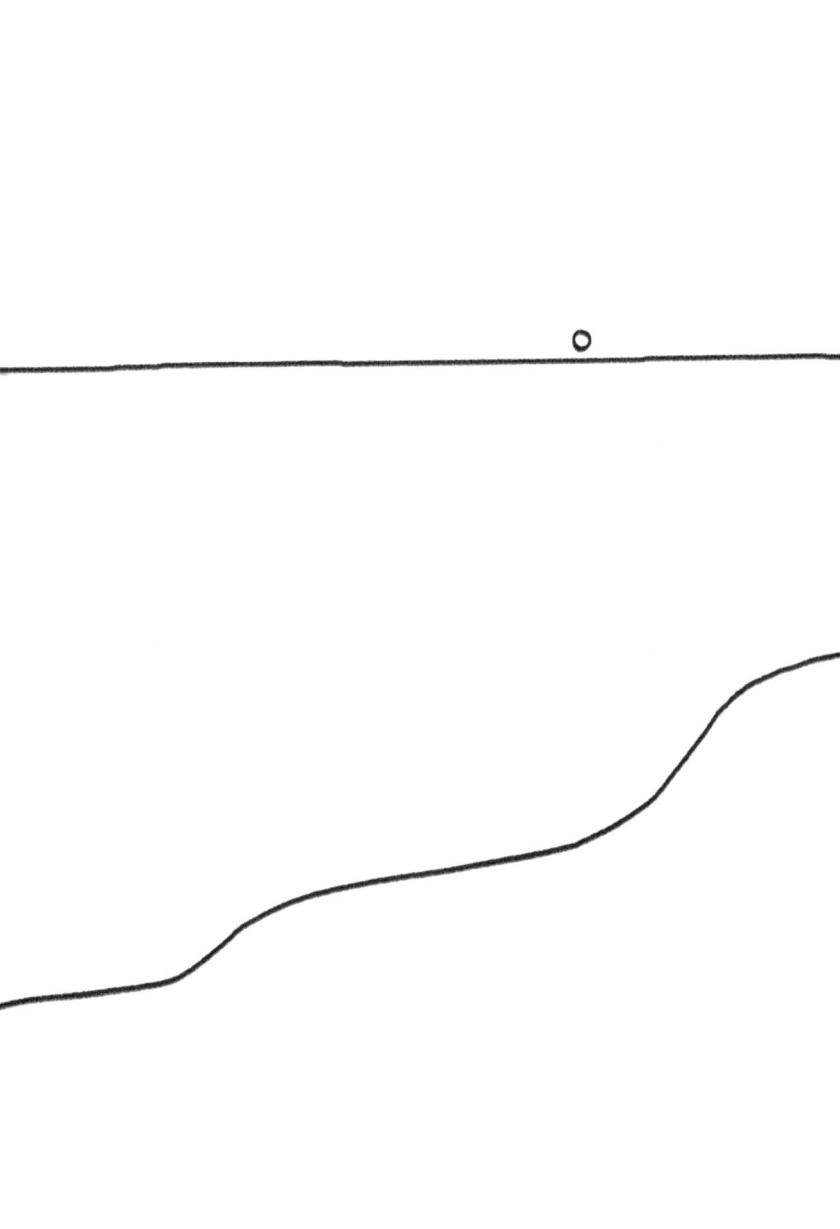

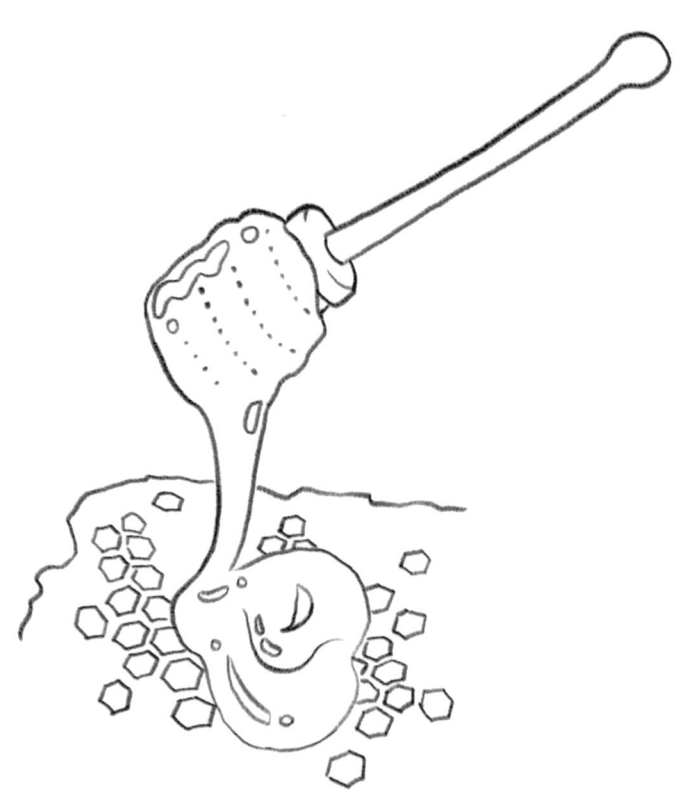

foraged

slower
slower
slower

like
the pace
of honey

gleaming

with it's
luxuriant
flow
of time

foraged

i
paint
what i
am

i cannot paint
what i
am not
yet

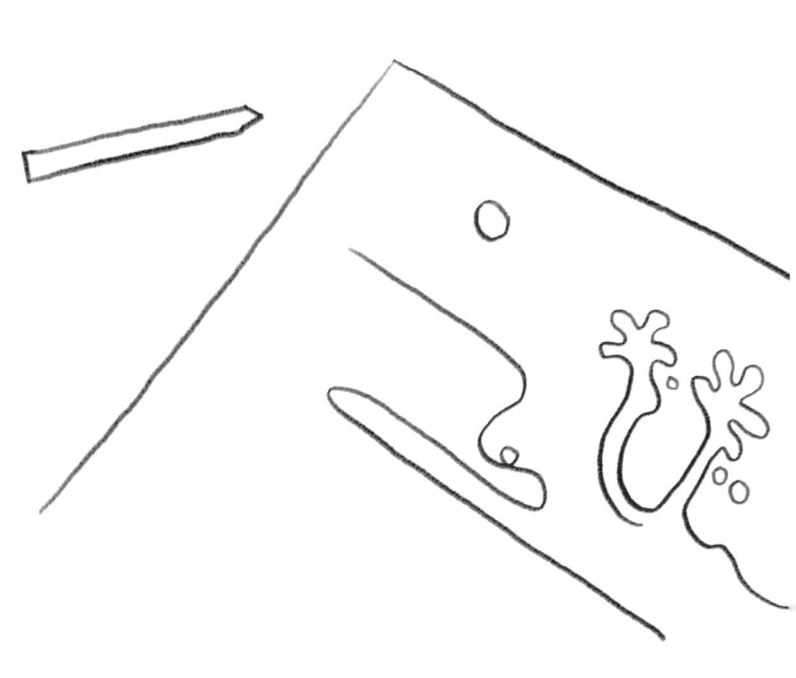

foraged

how to be
an artist:

try

again again again again again again again again again again again
again again again again again again again again again again again
again again again again again again again again again again again
again again again again again again again again again again again
again again again again again again again again again again again
again again again again again again again again again again again
again again again again again again again again again again again
again again again again again again again again again again again
again again again again again again again again again again again
again again again again again again again again again again again
again again again again again again again again again again again
again again again again again again again again again again again
again again again again again again again again again again again
again again again again again again again again again again again
again again again again again again again again again again again
again again again again again again again again again again again
again again again again again again again again again again again
again again again again again again again again again again again
again again again again again again again again again again again
again again again again again again again again again again again
again again again again again again again again again again again
again again again again again again again again again again again
again again again again again again again again again again again
again again again again again again again again again again again
again again again again again again again again again again again
again again again again again again again again again again again
again again again again again again again again again again again
again again again again again again again again again again again
again again again again again again again again again again again
again again again again again again again again again again again
again again again again again again again again again again again
again again again again again again again again again again again
again again again again again again again again again again again
again again again again again again again again again again again
again again again again again again again again again again again
again again again again again again again again again again again
again again again again again again again again again again again
again again again again again again again again again again again
again again again again again again again again again again again
again again again again again again again again again again again

foraged

i give myself
to the work

i succumb
to the labor

i birth
the art

or does it
birth
me?

foraged

create
create
create
create

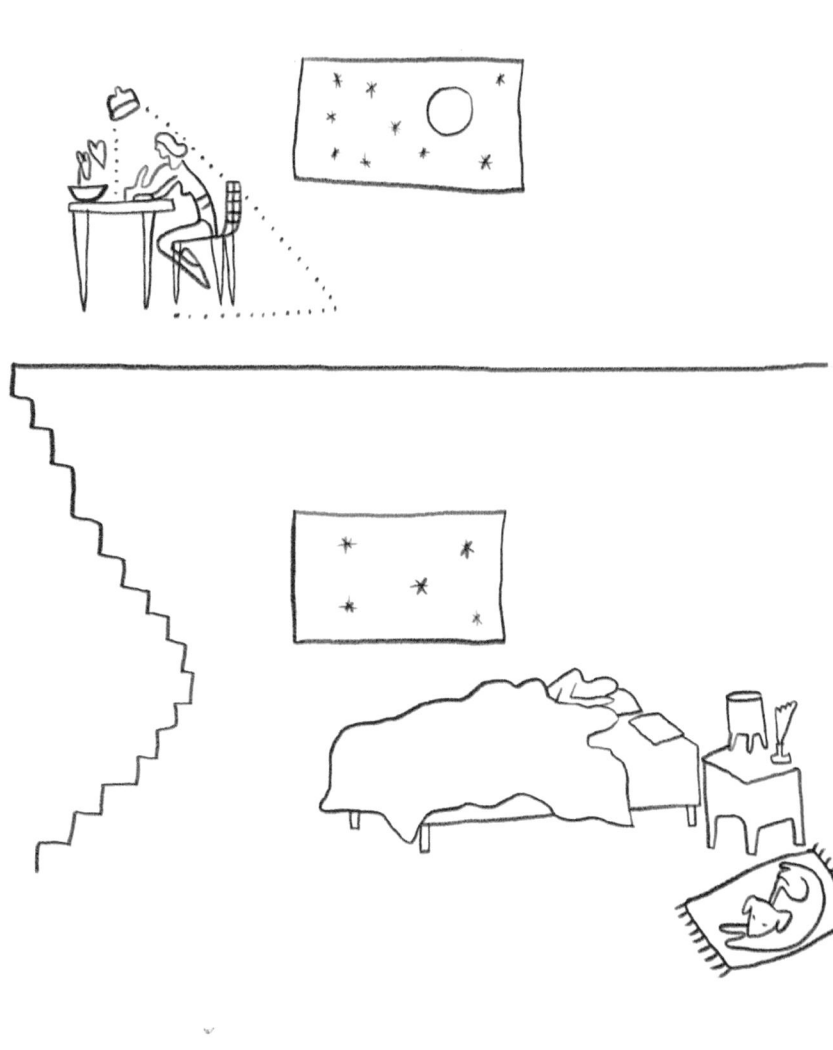

foraged

i must
be
loyal
to the
idea

sacred duty

foraged

art  flows
out of me

but it is
not meant
to stay
here

foraged

i
want
to be
an
observer
of the
natural
world

an art, a science

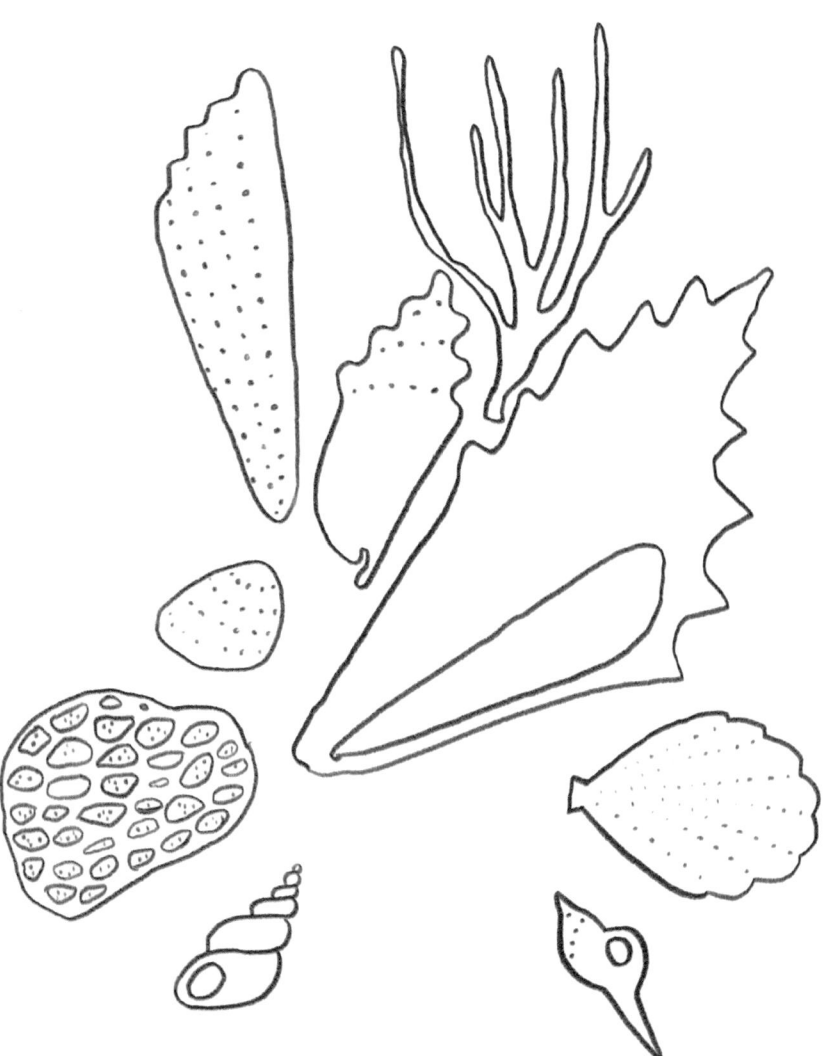

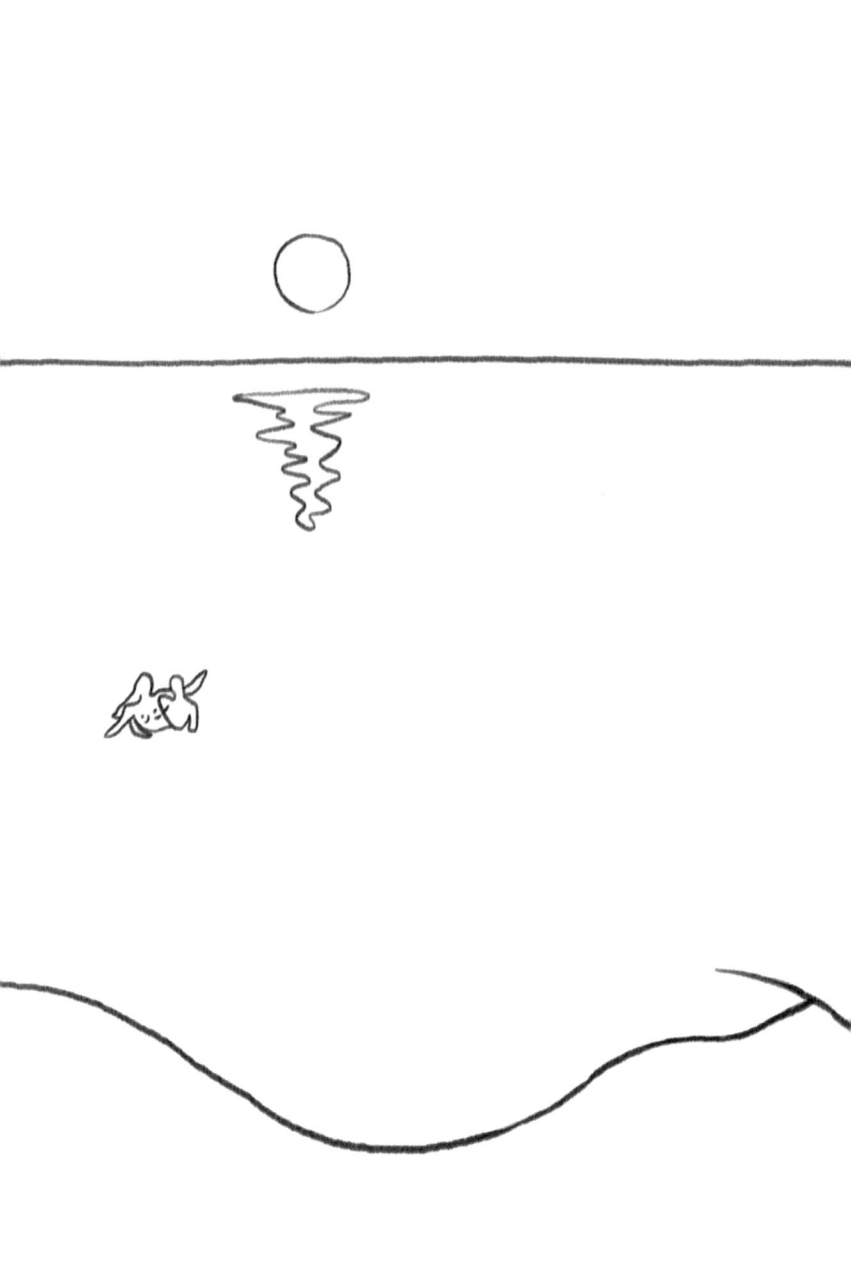

foraged

how quickly
i return
to myself
in
wild places

foraged

meditation

foraged

like the rain
from the
dark ominous
clouds

it overflows
out of us

so that we too
might feel
that earth scented
cleansing

that lightness
of the load

that quiet
healing
within

deluge

foraged

as i step
into the sea

i am reminded
to dive
deeply
into this
abundance

if what i can see
seems like infinity

maybe it also
can be true
for me

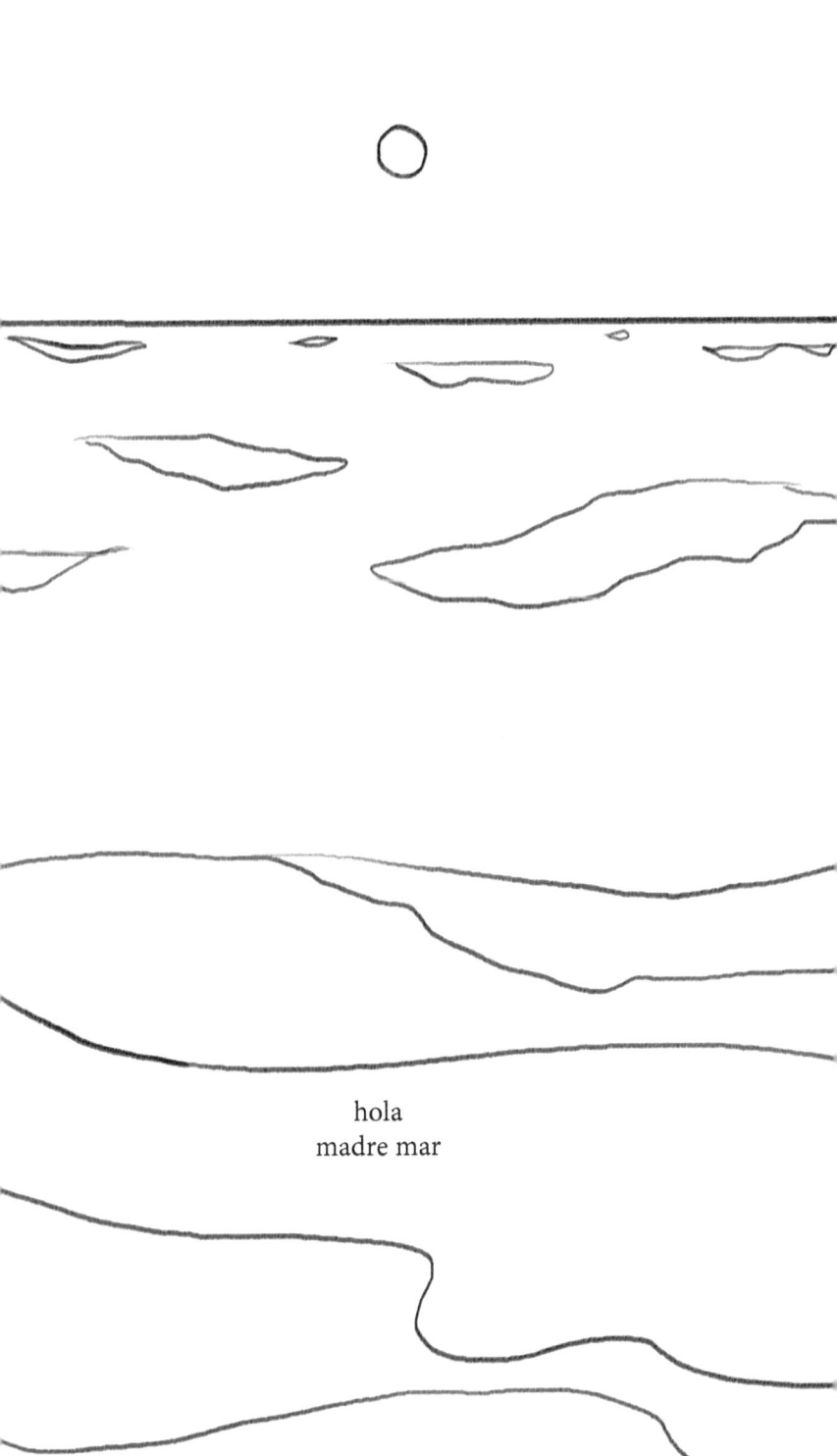

hola
madre mar

foraged

the ocean
steadily roars
throwing itself
against
sand and stone

i was awakened
by the sound

and the moon's gaze
beckoned me
into the
night

which,
as i am drawn
into the
darkness

i see is only
filled with
light

dark + luminous

foraged

admiring this
wild earth
is my path
home
to you

the call

foraged

it's almost as if
some benevolence
exists out there
just beyond
my sight

foraged


with my ear
pressed to the earth

i listen for
notes that ring true

that harmonize
with my
deep knowing

and i will not
discriminate

based on
from
where it comes

no matter how
surprising the
source

no matter how
unusual
the form

quantum
entanglement
gives me
much hope

if space and time
are illusions

there is much more
unexplored
possibility of

connection + community

in ways
previously thought
impossible

a quantum belonging

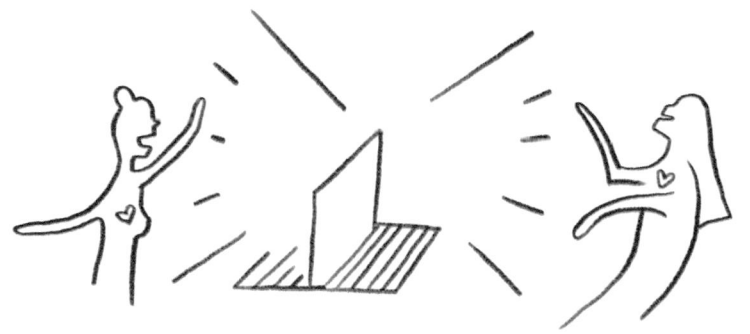

worm hole

foraged

i have been
near + apart
from people i love
all my life

and yet
here they are
within me

foraged

if we really do
live in an
observer universe

how necessary
how sacred
how right

to watch
the wonder
of this
wild world

unfolding
before our
eyes

observing our duties

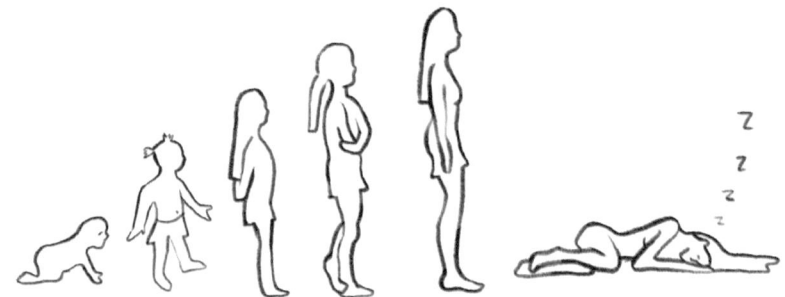

foraged

by now
i have been
at least

five

different
people
in my life

i feel
tired
from all this
becoming

if what i
once have
known
can change

(if i can change)

if everything
is moving

everything in flux

then how
do i
know

where i am
at all?

(dis)orientation

maybe i have
never been
certain of
anything

foraged

there
will

( always )

be
space

to
change
your
mind

foraged

all i have
is my perception

so i must
trust
that somehow
i can perceive

i observe beauty
may beauty abound

i observe peace
may peace abound

i observe abundance
may abundance abound

foraged

if our
observations
actually affect
existence

then by
pausing to smell
a flower

did i
beckon it
to exist?

could it be
could it be
could it be

that it was there
all along
just for me?

a scented question

foraged

i attune
my eyes
to beauty

foraged

this is the
endless
work

foraged

i want to
witness
every drop
of beauty
in this
life

foraged




i want
to be
so
thoroughly

grateful

that not
a speck
escapes
my
gaze

foraged

i
want
to
dive
so
deep

into
this
sweet
sea of
gratitude

foraged

i want
to

dive
deeper

into this
life

and descend
into this
ever changing
present

foraged




a craving for
cold
dark waters

silent and soothing

the deepest blue
calls to me

glimmering and
mysterious

a longing
both without
and within

beckoning me
deeper

like
a moth
to a flame

i dive
deeper
in

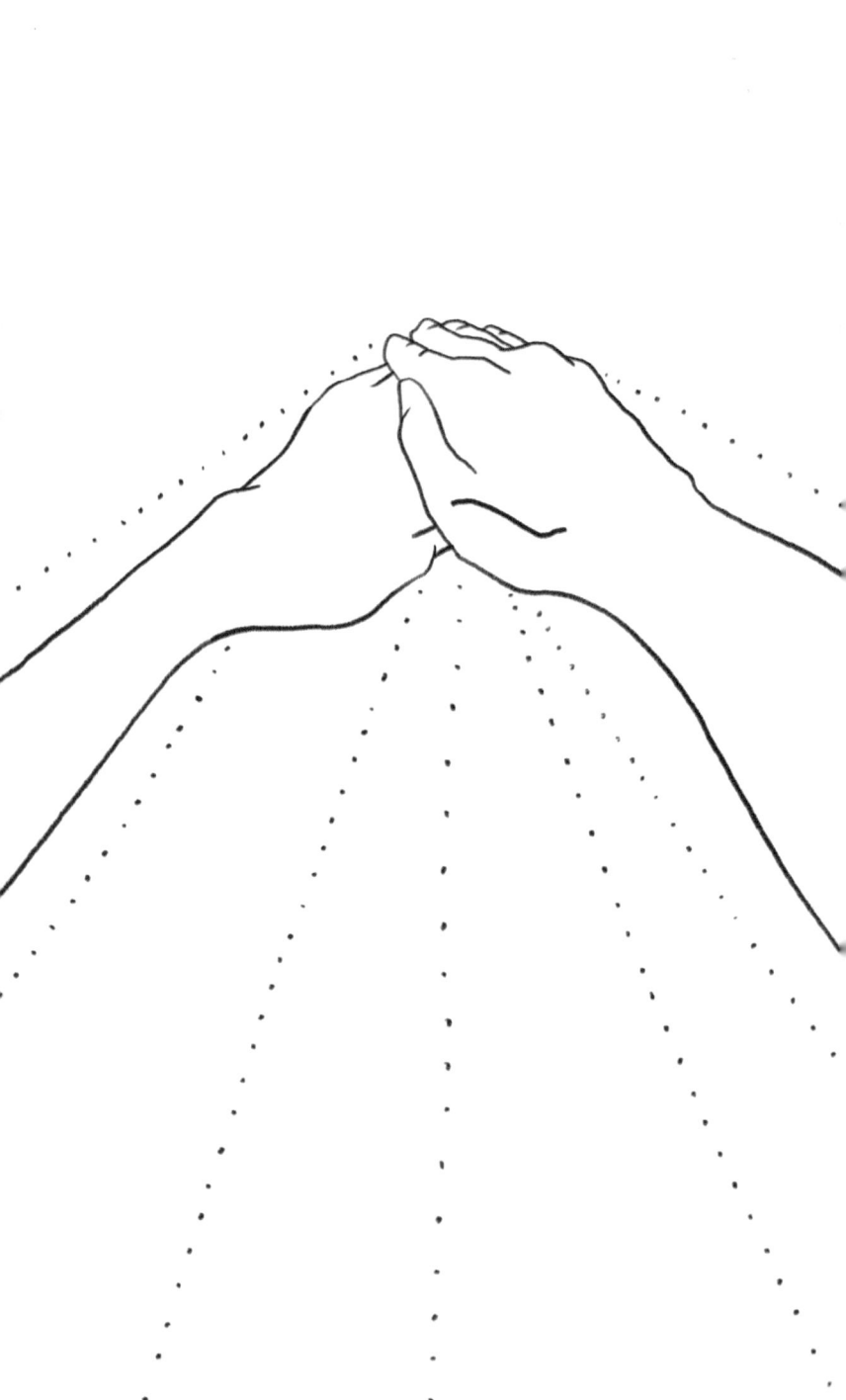

foraged

the descent is the prayer

foraged

succumbing
to this
subterranean
flow

i trust my sight

i trust my instinct

and i

dive

more

deeply

within

down here
in the deep blue
there is something
soul quenching
in the quiet cool pressure
holding me

but i cannot stay
as long as i wish

and even when
i'm here
i'm so limited
by my anxious
inhale

seemly always
limited by

my capacity
my endurance
my ability

to hold space


meditation / free dive

foraged

i want
to dive
so deep

i don't know
if i will
ever
come back
up
for air

foraged

life is
so
much more

forgiving

than i was
ever told

foraged

i would never
trade
my mistakes

for a
clean record

from them
i have learned

everything
everything
everything

they are
precious
to me

foraged

and i hope to fail and grow exquisitely

.

foraged

nothing is wasted

like the earth
everything is
composted

renewed

matter only
changes form

so who will you
become

again and again and again

foraged

my spirituality
is a
pandora's box

everything is
outside

and there
is not
much left
indoors

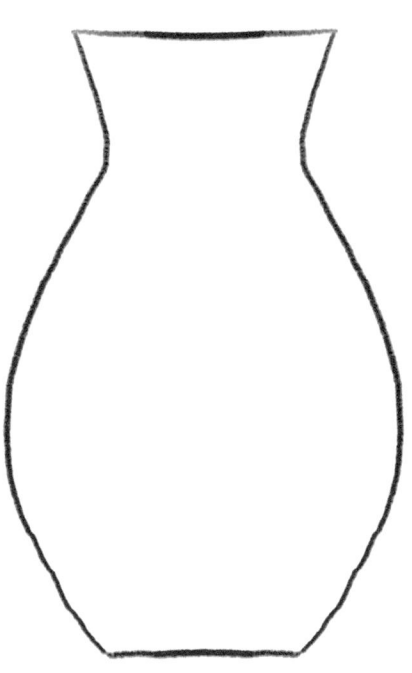

foraged




i watch
the sunrise
as a prayer

the moon rise
as a ritual

i swim
in the sea
religiously

the earth
has always been
the first
holy place

everything
has always
ever been
sacred




on earth as it is

foraged

draw
near to
the lord

and he will
draw
near to
you

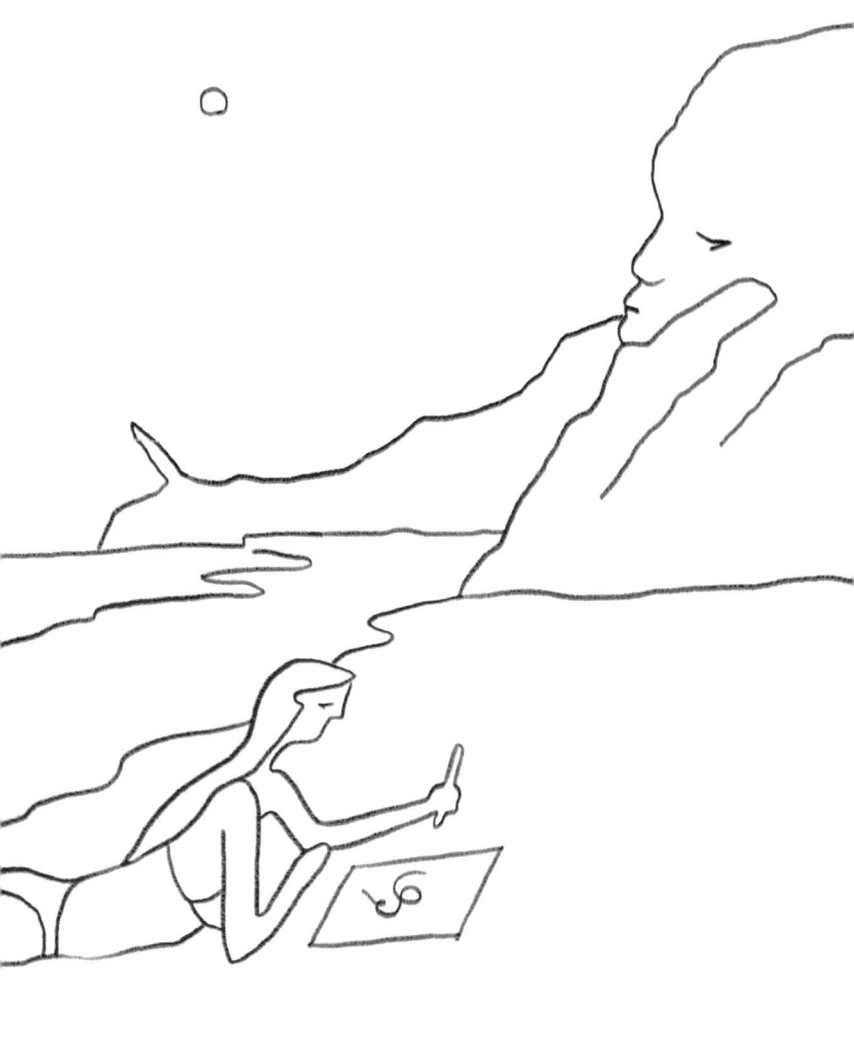

i renounce
temples
and churches
and man made
structures

i lose myself
in the
everlasting rhythm
of the earth

the tides of the sea
the cycles of the moon
the seasons of the earth

here i know
who i am

coming from everything

brief and dazzling

and shortly
to everything

i will again
return

speaking in tongues
casting out demons
gold flakes falling from heaven
visions and prophecies

just another mundane
weekend of my
childhood,
but i never witnessed
any miracles

they told me
i needed
to have faith

and you know,
they weren't wrong

i never did
have much faith
in a show biz god

one that needed
smoke and mirrors
and little tricks

one that kept
count of converts

ah, no thank you
i do not need
anything
out of the ordinary

really, the ordinary
is almost too miraculous
for me:

the way the earth
sustains our lives

the complex balance
of ecosystems

death and decay
as the catalyst for
new life

the unfailing rhythm of
the sun, earth, moon and stars

i don't need any
signs or signals

i know my place
here,
out in the wild

the ordinary is pretty extra, to me

foraged

whenever i try
to write about
god

my words
turn into
nature songs

foraged

god
so loved
this earth

that they gave their
one and only
sun

so that
everyone
who honored
the land
and every being
upon it

would have
an everlasting
and symbiotic
ecosystem

gospel

foraged

i can
no longer
pay the price
of acceptance

at the
expense
of being my
fullest
self

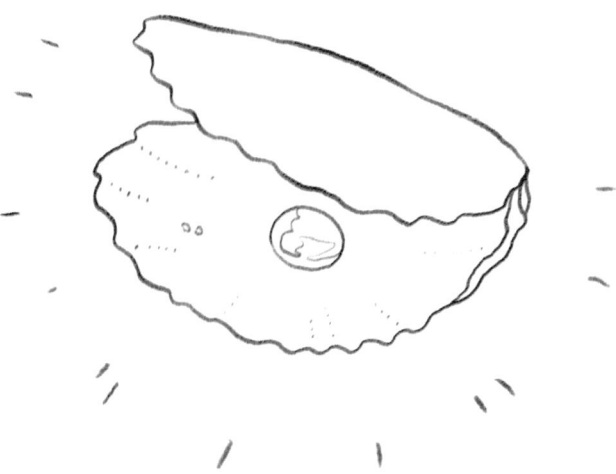

the pearl of great price (is me)

foraged

i had to
let go
of religion
to stay
connected
to the
source

or

i had to
let go
of the source
to stay
connected
to
religion

conscientious objector

foraged

i
trust fall
into the
oceanic
mystery

knowing
that
at it's
depth

it is play
it is joy
it is love

me, a mystic

foraged

collect all of your loves

even the smallest joy

laugh cry smile sing create

forgive forgive forgive

this is the balm

foraged

i read that the
ancients
believed
you could
dream your
own cure

foraged




i have been
dreaming about

sunset colored
pastel clouds

shells
smooth giant
glossy and
iridescent

flowers flowers
blooming
infused in
scented oil

can my healing
truly
be this
lovely

foraged

everything
is unfolding
at exactly
the right
time

rest

foraged

i was
taught
that

healing
forgiveness
peace
love

were outsourced

that the
deepest truth
about me

was my
darkness

foraged

i have
found
that

healing
forgiveness
peace
love

come from within

that the
deepest truth
about me

is my
light

foraged

i could have
waited

an eternity

for
someone else
to save me

foraged

but i have
become
my own
best
healer

a foraged cure

foraged

remember
your way
back home
to yourself

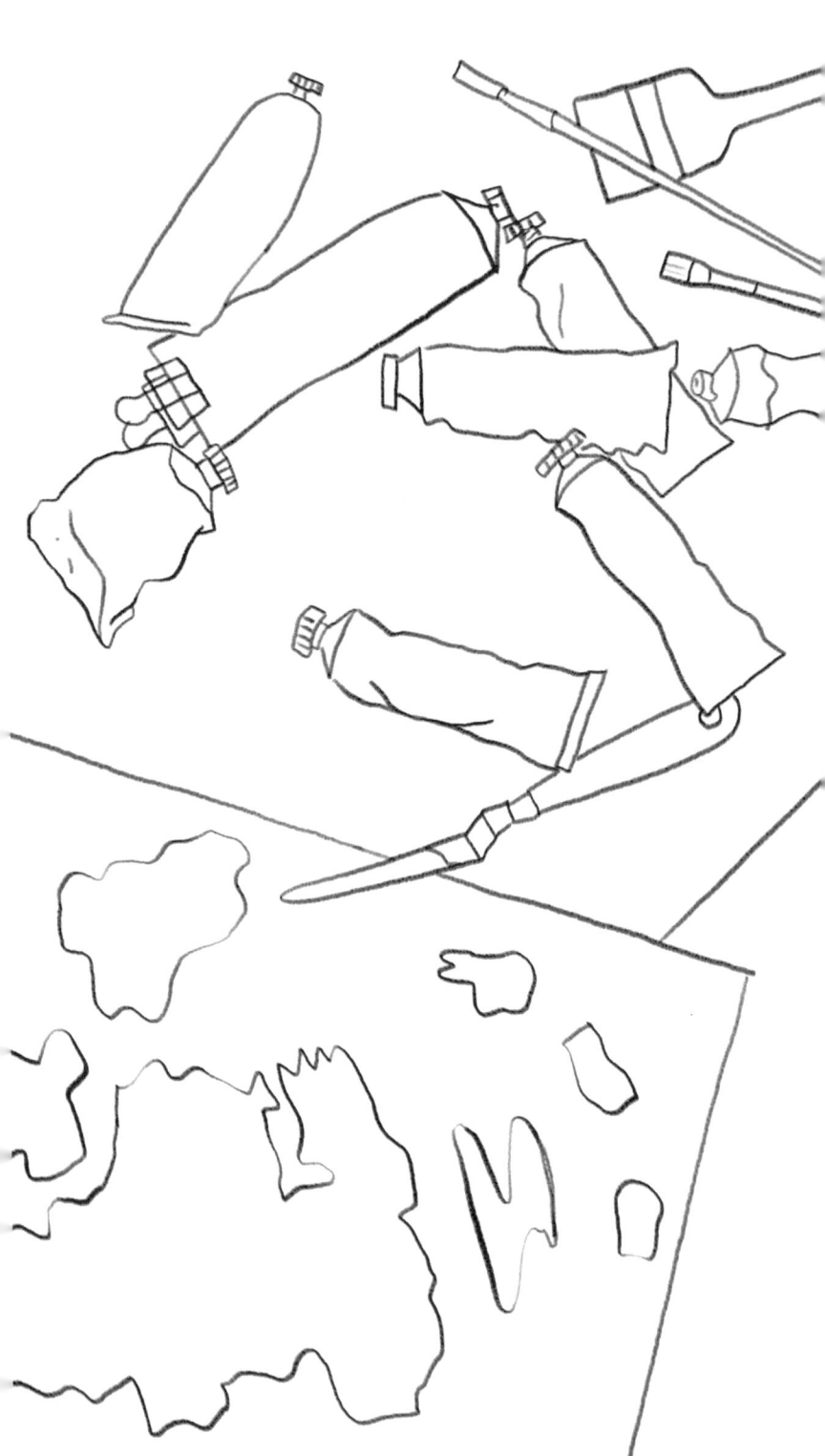

may my life
be my
greatest
work of
art

foraged

i want
to live out
my
wildest
dreams

foraged

and
dream
new
dreams

About the Author

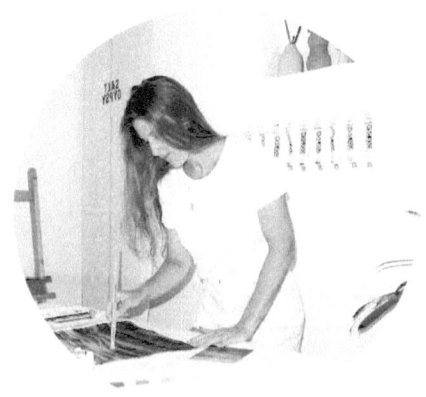

Rachel Sierra grew up in the Caribbean and South America, and travel has been a central part of her life. As a self-taught painter and multidisciplinary creative, her work has been displayed in galleries and in print internationally. When she's not painting in her studio, you'll find her surfing, diving, or otherwise outside. She is driven to document life in any way - whether by painting, film photography, or writing poetry.

RACHELSIERRAART.COM

@rachel.sierra.art

.